CONSTITUTIONAL CONVENTION
OF STATES
(America's Plan for Survival)

HANK SIMS

ISBN-13: 9781514377390
ISBN-10: 151437739X

ALSO BY HANK SIMS

AMERICA'S CHANCE FOR SURVIVAL
(WHAT I BELIEVE)
(Published in 2009)

AMERICA'S PLAN FOR SURVIVAL
(Published in 2014)

The author may be contacted at: apfsbook@aol.com

This book is dedicated to all those who are concerned about the survival of our Country.

Credits

My thanks go to Mr. David Dietrich, Mr. Gary Porter and Carroll Childers for their considered edits and additions.

Also, those who contributed to and endorsed my book America's Plan for Survival which is the basis for this writing:

MG (Ret) Carroll Childers
Greg Browne, British Citizen
Paul Burgener, FairTax Proponent
Les Sims, retired Boeing Executive
Larry Gentry, retired Arkansas State Police Sergeant

Endorsements

"If only America would read this, we would all be better off," Carroll D. Childers P.E., Major General USARNG, Ranger (Retired)

THE FOUNDING FATHERS WERE WISE MEN
BUT, AMERICA IS NOT FOLLOWING
THEIR INTENT

THIS BOOK PROPOSES NO CHANGES
NOR AMENDMENTS TO THE CONSTITUTION
BUT THOSE TO CAUSE ENFORCEMEMT
TO BE CLOSER TO THE INTENT
OF THE FOUNDERS

THIS BOOK DOES PROPOSE AMENDMENTS
THAT THE AUTHOR DESIRES, AND
ALTERNATIVE WORDING, FOR CONSIDERATION
BY DELEGATES TO THE CONVENTION

FOREWORD

This book is a follow-up of my heart-felt book, "America's Plan for Survival." I refer the reader to that book for the backup for thoughts summarized here. This book is intended to go directly to the issues. The Table of Contents of "America's Plan for Survival" is at Annex I, for reference.

America has lost the vision of our Founding Fathers. Correction of the course of our country is essential if the country is to survive.

> "I predict future happiness for Americans if they can prevent the government from wasting the labors of the people under the pretense of taking care of them." Thomas Jefferson.

The Constitution allows for amendments to the Constitution in Article V. It allows two methods: the first is when initiated by Congress; the second is when called by the States. The only amendments made, to date, have followed the first approach. But since Congress is complicit in the current problems, the only real hope is the second method, the Convention of the States.

The best thing that could happen would be that our Federal government implement (enforce) the Constitution as intended by the founders without going beyond their intent. But, since we cannot trust our current Federal government to enforce the Constitution, the only alternative is a COS, as defined in Article V of the Constitution.

Troubles with the existing Confederation of States finally encouraged Madison and Hamilton to request a convention of the states, ostensibly to discuss navigation issues on the Potomac. Meeting in Annapolis in September 1786, the five delegations which attended suggested to the states and to Congress that a "Grand Convention" meet in Philadelphia the following May. By February 1787, when Congress finally endorsed the plan, seven states had already selected and instructed their delegates to recommend changes to the Articles that would "render the Constitution of the Federal Government adequate to the exigencies of the Union."

The convention instead resulted in a completely new Constitution, the Constitution we now have.

Two methods for amending the new Constitution were incorporated in the document:

Article V

The Congress, whenever *two thirds of both Houses* shall deem it necessary, shall propose *Amendments* **to this Constitution**, or, on the Application of the Legislatures of **two thirds of the several States**, shall call a Convention for proposing Amendments, which, in either Case, shall be valid to all Intents and Purposes, as Part of this Constitution, when ratified by the Legislatures of *three fourths of the several States* or by Conventions in three fourths thereof...

The founding fathers were wise men, well read in the problems of the world. They wrote a Constitution that they believed would guide the country well into the future. They understood that circumstances would change. Therefore, they made provisions that the Constitution could be changed, but only with care. All three branches of our government have deviated from the Constitution by Presidential executive orders, Congressional overreach and legislating from the Bench; all without amending the Constitution.

The founding fathers intended that the people would govern. They envisioned a Republic with leaders selected by an "informed population."

I believe we should be concerned about the survival of our country instead of the marginal benefits of universal health care, government subsidies and grants, and political correctness.

In order to survive as a country, I believe we must begin with the following actions:

1) Strengthen the Constitution by amendment.
2) Reduce spending and repay the National Debt.
3) Revise the tax code.
4) Return to limited government and free market economy.
5) Elect leaders that are competent and representative.
6) Return the Balance of Power among Branches of Government.

The original Constitution and Bill or Rights have guided our country. However, amendments have sometimes been added without proper consideration (our current politicians are not as wise as were the founders).

"The Constitution was made to guard the people against the dangers of good intentions."
Daniel Webster

The Constitution (with my suggested revisions/Amendments clearly annotated) is included. I sincerely believe that every American should read and understand this document. I am sorely disappointed that so few who have.

Convention of States:

We must convene a Convention of the States (COS), the second method authorized by Article V.

Article V of the Constitution allows for a convention for proposing Amendments. If two thirds of the states apply to Congress for a convention, Congress <u>shall</u> call for the convention. If three quarters of the states ratify proposed amendments, they are approved, and that approval is not reversible by the federal government.

The Constitution gives no guidance as to how the convention will be managed. State legislatures may certainly give strict instructions to their selected delegates and retain recall authority. After convening, the Convention of the States must be without restriction, as was the convention of 1787. The simple fact is that once the convention assembles, it cannot be directed by outside authority.

Actions are underway for just such an event; however, previous state initiatives have been un-coordinated. Some states have applied for a convention for a single subject, such as a Balanced Budget Amendment. However the wording of the applications has varied widely.

Recognizing that many of these needed actions are not in the self-interest of our current legislators, delegates to the COS should not hold any elective office and should forswear future political ambitions. This is to ensure that the COS determinations will reflect the desires of the people, not professional politicians.

My recommendations of subjects and actions are as follows:

1) Reinstitute the Balance of Power. Each of the branches, Executive, Legislative and Judicial should review all actions of the other branches. When one branch challenges an action of another, the third branch will be the arbitrator. A simple majority of the arbitrator will be final.

   The President will enforce the Constitution and all Federal Laws.
   SCOTUS will examine and judge all Federal laws and executive orders.
   Congress will make all Federal laws.

2) Enforce the Ninth Amendment. No government, Federal or State will dictate citizen actions that do not impact on others.

3) Enforce limited government:

   Eliminate the Departments of Energy, Education and Health and Human Services. These agencies have no Constitutional basis and their functions should appropriately be accomplished by the States or the Free Market.

   Establish an agency in all departments for systematic review of current and past laws, actions and departments for constitutionality, obsolescence and efficiency. These agencies should eliminate established departments' ability to make regulations that bear the weight of law.

   The Departments of Justice, Labor and Commerce (All Departments) should be carefully reviewed to ensure that their functions are Constitutional and applicable to all Americans, not specific elements.

   Eliminate duplicative programs among all departments.

9

Eliminate (phase out) most (all?) subsidies, grants and rebates to States, institutions and individuals.

> "The national budget must be balanced.
> The public debt must be reduced. The arrogance of the authorities must be moderated and controlled.
> Payments to foreign governments must be reduced, if the nation doesn't want to go bankrupt.
> People must again learn to work, instead of living on public assistance."
> Cicero

4) Ensure the Integrity of the Vote:

Ensure citizenship of voters.

Re-institute a poll test and increase the voting age to ensure intelligence and experience of the voter. We must recognize that the establishment, the media and legislators, manipulate the vote of uninformed voters.

> "Democracy requires an informed population."
> Thomas Jefferson.

5) Ensure that the current Article II, Section 1 and Twelfth Amendment approach to electing the President and Vice-President is followed.

> "The Electors will meet in their respective states and vote by ballot for the President and Vice-President...they shall name in their ballots the person voted for as President, and in distinct ballots the person voted for as Vice-President...and transmit...to the President of the Senate..." [Amendment XII]. Electors will not be committed to specific candidates prior to that meeting.
>
> The founders wrote it this way to ensure that electors will be informed on the issues and the candidates.

9) Revise the Tax Code. Implement the FairTax. Eliminate income taxes and corporate taxes and import jobs that have been lost to overseas businesses.

10) Re-establish our Congressmen as representatives of the people rather than professional politicians.

Reduce numbers of Congressmen and Senators to reduce cost and confusion in managing 535 legislators. One senator per state and 100 (possibly as many as 150) representatives based on population should be adepuate and more representative. The Founding Fathers could not have imagined 435 Congressmen.

"We hang the petty thieves and appoint the great ones to public office." Aesop

Return the Senate to State control by repealing the 17th Amendment.

Institute Term Limits.

11) Limit all laws to 25 pages and one subject so that Congressmen and voters can understand the proposed law.

"We must pass this bill [Obamacare] so we can, Ah, see what's in it." Nancy Pelosi

"It will be of little avail to the people, that the laws are made by men of their own choice, if the laws be so voluminous that they cannot be read, or so incoherent that they cannot be understood" James Madison, Federalist NO. 62

12) Make all actions equally applicable to all states and citizens, including government officials.

Amend the General Welfare clause to require that all actions apply only to all Americans.

SPECIFIC CONSTITUTIONAL RECOMMENDATIONS:

Specific changes to the Constitution are listed below but certain clarifications are annotated on the full text of the Constitution, included below.

Term Limits.

Revise the 22nd Amendment to read: "No person shall be elected to any federal office more than once, with a term of six years. (Alternative wording "Include two four year terms for President, two six year terms for Senator and four two year terms for Representative." But my feeling is that a single term eliminates maneuvering and deal making in order to get re-elected).

"As a newly-elected US Senator, your first
and most important job is to get, of all things, re-elected"
Zell Miller

Amend the Constitution to establish a maximum term of 20 years and maximum age of 80 for Federal Justices including members of the Supreme Court. (An alternative is to have a six year term with a limit on one re-appointment by the President that is in office at the time of the re-appointment.) Either option is an improvement

Numbers in Congress. Revise the Constitution, Article I, Section 2 to allow for one Senator per state and 100 (or 150) Representatives based on population; each State will have at least one Representative. (Alternative wording "Revise the Constitution, Article I, Section 2 to allow for two

Senators per state and 150 (or 200) Representatives based on population; each State will have at least two Representatives.

Clarify Article II, Section 1 to clearly state that "Natural Born" means born of two parents that are US Citizens at the time of birth and having resided in the United States for 14 years.

Repeal Amendment XVI. Eliminate the IRS, and income tax; use FairTax or another alternative with similar characteristics but no tax on income.

Repeal Amendment XVII. It violates Article IV, Section 4 and the Tenth Amendment; return the Senate to State control.

Modify Amendment XXVI, Change voting age to 25 years to ensure greater maturity. A younger age may be appropriate if combined with a Poll Test.

Add: Amendment XXVIII, Voter Integrity.

Repeal the Voting Rights Act of 1965 and revise the Constitution to require a test of all voters and positive proof of US Citizenship.

Add: Amendment XXIX, Balance of Power.

Each of the branches, Executive, Legislative and Judicial should review all actions of the other branches. When one branch challenges an action of another, the third branch will be the arbitrator. A simple majority of the arbitrator will be final.

<u>Add: Amendment XXX</u>.

Federal Justices including members of the Supreme Court will have a maximum term of 20 years and maximum age of 80 years of age. (Alternative wording, "Federal Justices including Supreme Court justices will be appointed to a term of 6 years, with a limit of one re-appointment by the appointing authority in office at the time of the re-appointment.")

DISCUSSION

Limited terms of office will foster a representative government instead of professional politicians.

Fewer Congressmen would eliminate most congressional districts, gerrymandering and much political maneuvering. I believe that fewer Congressmen would *improve* representation of the people; it would make decision making easier and reduce political maneuvering. As a bonus, it would reduce costs and do away with most gerrymandering.

A Poll Test may prevent the coming suicide of our republic. Of course there is difficulty in deciding who should write the test; this can be overcome. The US Citizenship Test (or a randomly selected sample of questions therefrom) should be a valid test and not subject to partisan issues.

A Poll Test is <u>not</u> prohibited by the Constitution. The Constitution does not mention qualifications for voting, it only specifies certain characteristics that may not be used to prevent a citizen from voting; by exclusion it left this right to the discretion of the States. As part of the civil rights movement in the 1960's the Voting Rights Act of 1965 made a poll test illegal. The law should be repealed. The Voting Rights Act in itself may well be unconstitutional.

Laws are too long to be understood by legislators who enact them and too long for the people impacted to readily understand. Laws should be limited to one subject so that politically motivated issues are not hidden within the law. A 25-page limit seems reasonable.

We should return to limited government and free market economy.

We should enforce the Balance of Power as envisioned by the founders.

I believe these changes to the Constitution will bring it closer to the intents of the Founding Fathers.

In this book, I provide a list of potential amendments for the delegates to the convention to consider.

I can almost guarantee that if none of these actions are taken, it will be the end of our nation, as we know it.

I can almost guarantee that if all these actions are taken, our nation will survive.

If part, but not all actions are taken, we have a chance.

THE US CONSTITUTION

The Constitution is the main subject of this book. I have added italics or highlighted certain places for emphasis.

I have made suggested changes on the document consistent with earlier discussion. I have ~~marked through~~ things I feel should be deleted and made suggested additions in parentheses, e.g. **(ADDED....) in bold text.** I have placed selected other portions that I feel are most important or that may be violated in bold text for emphasis.

Knowing these edits, you can safely read the original content. Also, I believe everyone needs to read and understand the Constitution.

THE CONSTITUTION OF THE UNITED STATES

WE THE PEOPLE of the United States, in Order to form a more perfect Union, establish Justice, insure domestic Tranquility, provide for the common defense, promote the general Welfare, and secure the Blessings of Liberty to ourselves and our Posterity, do ordain and establish this Constitution for the United States of America.

Article. I.

Section. 1. *All legislative Powers herein granted shall be vested in a Congress* of the United States **(ADDED: Neither the President nor Supreme Court will make laws),** which shall consist of a Senate and House of Representatives.

Section. 2. The *House of Representatives* shall be composed of Members chosen *every second* Year **(ADDED: for a SINGLE term of 6 years)** by the People of the several States, and the Electors in each State shall have the Qualifications requisite for Electors of the most numerous Branch of the State Legislature.

No Person shall be a Representative who shall not have attained the Age of twenty five Years, and been seven Years a Citizen of the United States, and who shall not, when elected, be an Inhabitant of that State in which he shall be chosen.

[Representatives and direct *Taxes shall be apportioned among the several States which may be included within this Union, according to their respective Numbers*, which shall be determined by adding to the whole Number of free Persons, including those bound to Service for a Term of Years, and excluding Indians not taxed, three fifths of all other Persons.][1] The actual Enumeration shall be made within three Years after the first Meeting of the Congress of the United States, and within every subsequent Term of ten Years, in such Manner as they shall by Law direct. The Number of Representatives shall not exceed **one (ADDED: hundred with a minimum of one per State)** ~~for every thirty~~ **Thousand,** but each State shall have at Least one Representative; and until such enumeration shall be made, the State of New Hampshire shall be entitled to chuse three, Massachusetts eight, Rhode-Island and Providence Plantations one, Connecticut five, New-York six, New Jersey four, Pennsylvania eight, Delaware one, Maryland six, Virginia ten, North Carolina five, South Carolina five, and Georgia three.

When vacancies happen in the Representation from any State, the Executive Authority thereof shall issue Writs of Election to fill such Vacancies.

The House of Representatives shall chuse their Speaker and other Officers; and shall have the sole *Power of Impeachment.*

Section. 3. *The **Senate** of the United States **shall be composed of** ~~two~~ **(ADDED: one) Senators from each State, [chosen by the Legislature]**[2] thereof for **(ADDED: a single term of) six Years;** and each Senator shall have one Vote.*

Immediately after they shall be assembled in Consequence of the first Election, they shall be divided as equally as may be into three Classes. The Seats of the Senators of the first Class shall be vacated at the Expiration of the second Year, of the second Class at the Expiration of the fourth Year, and of the third Class at the Expiration of the sixth Year, so that one third may be chosen every second Year; [and if Vacancies happen by Resignation, or otherwise, during Recess of the Legislature of any State, the Executive thereof may make temporary Appointments until the next Meeting of the Legislature, which shall then fill such Vacancies].[3]

No Person shall be a Senator who shall not have attained to the Age of thirty Years, and been nine Years a Citizen of the United States, and who shall not, when elected, be an Inhabitant of that State for which he shall be chosen.

The Vice President of the United States shall be President of the Senate, but shall have no Vote, unless they be equally divided.

The Senate shall chuse their other Officers, and also a President pro tempore, in the Absence of the Vice President, or when he shall exercise the Office of President of the United States.

The Senate shall have the sole Power to *try all Impeachments*. When sitting for that Purpose, they shall be on Oath or Affirmation. When the President of the United States is tried, the Chief Justice shall preside: And no Person shall be convicted without the Concurrence of two thirds of the Members present.

Judgment in Cases of Impeachment shall not extend further than to removal from Office, and disqualification to hold and enjoy any Office of honor, Trust or Profit under the United States: but the Party convicted shall nevertheless be liable and subject to Indictment, Trial, Judgment and Punishment, according to Law.

Section. 4. The Times, Places and Manner of holding *Elections for Senators and Representatives, shall be prescribed in each State by the Legislature thereof*; but the Congress may at any time by law make or alter such Regulations, except as to the Places of chusing Senators.

The Congress shall assemble at least [sic] once in every Year, and such Meeting shall [be on the first Monday in December,]⁴ unless they shall by Law appoint a different Day.

Section. 5. Each House shall be the Judge of the Elections, Returns and Qualifications of its own Members, and a Majority of each shall constitute a Quorum to do Business; but a smaller Number may adjourn from day to day, and may be authorized to compel the Attendance of absent Members, in such Manner, and under such Penalties as each House may provide.

Each House shall keep a Journal of its Proceedings, and from time to time publish the same, excepting such Parts as may in their Judgment require Secrecy; and the Yeas and Nays of the Members of either House on any question shall, at the Desire of one fifth of those Present, be entered on the Journal.

Neither House, during the Session of Congress, shall, without the Consent of the other, adjourn for more than three days, nor to any other Place than that in which the two Houses shall be sitting.

Section. 6. The Senators and Representatives shall receive a Compensation for their Services, to be ascertained by law, and paid out of the Treasury of the United States. They shall in all Cases, except Treason, Felony and Breach of the Peace, be *privileged from Arrest* during their Attendance at the Session of their respective Houses, and in going to and returning from the same; and for any speech or Debate in either House, they shall not be questioned by any other Place.

No Senator or Representative shall, during the Time for which he was elected, be appointed to any civil Office under the Authority of the United States, which shall have been created, or the Emoluments whereof shall have been increased during such time; and no Person holding any Office under the United States, shall be a Member of either House during his Continuance in Office.

Section. 7. *All Bills for raising Revenue shall originate in the House of Representatives*; but the Senate may propose or concur with Amendments as on other Bills.

Every Bill which shall have passed the House of Representatives and the Senate, shall, before it become a Law, be presented to the President of the United States: If he approve he shall sign it, but if not he shall return it, with his Objections to the House in which it shall have originated, who shall enter the Objections at large on their Journal, and proceed to reconsider it. If after such Reconsideration two thirds of that House shall agree to pass the Bill, it shall be sent, together with the Objections, to the other House, by which it shall likewise be reconsidered, and if approved by two thirds of that House, it shall become a Law. But in all such Cases the Votes of both Houses shall be determined by yeas and Nays, and the Names of the Persons voting for and against the Bill shall be entered on the Journal of each House respectively. If any Bill shall not be returned by the President within ten Days (Sundays excepted) after it shall have been presented to him, the Same shall be a Law, in like Manner as if he had signed it, unless the Congress by the Adjournment prevent its Return, in which Case it shall not be a Law.

Every Order, Resolution, or Vote to which the Concurrence of the Senate and House of Representatives may be necessary (except on a question of Adjournment) shall be presented to the President of the United States; and before the Same shall take Effect, shall be approved by him, *or being disapproved by him, shall be repassed by two thirds of the Senate and House of Representatives*, according to the Rules and Limitations prescribed in the Case of a Bill.

Section. 8. The Congress shall have Power To lay and collect *Taxes,* Duties, Imposts and *Excises*, to pay the Debts and provide for the common Defence and ~~general~~ **[ADDED: Welfare of all inhabitants of the]** United States. **[ADDED: No expenditure may favor one group or class of citizens to the exclusion of others.]** ~~but al~~ All Duties, Imposts and *Excises **shall be uniform throughout the United States;***

To borrow Money on the credit of the United States;

To regulate Commerce with foreign Nations, and *among the several States*, and with the Indian Tribes;

To establish an uniform *Rule of Naturalization*, and uniform Laws on the subject of Bankruptcies throughout the United States;

To *coin Money*, regulate the Value thereof, and of foreign Coin, and fix the Standard of Weights and Measures;

To provide for the Punishment of counterfeiting the Securities and current Coin of the United States;

To establish *Post Offices* and post Roads;

To promote the Progress of Science and useful Arts, by securing for limited Times to *Authors and Inventors* the exclusive Right to their respective Writings and Discoveries;

To constitute Tribunals inferior to the supreme Court;

To define and punish Piracies and Felonies committed on the high Seas, and Offences against the Law of Nations;

To declare War, grant Letters of Marque and Reprisal, and make Rules concerning Captures on Land and Water;

To raise and support Armies, but no Appropriation of Money to that use shall be for a longer Term than two years;

To provide and maintain a Navy;

To make Rules for the Government and Regulation of the land and naval Forces;

To provide for calling forth the Militia to execute the Laws of the Union, suppress Insurrections and repel Invasions;

To provide for organizing, arming, and disciplining, the *Militia*, and for governing such Part of them as may be employed in the Service of the United States, reserving to the States respectively, the Appointment of the Officers, and the Authority of training the Militia according to the discipline prescribed by Congress;

To exercise exclusive Legislation in all Cases whatsoever, over such District (not exceeding ten Miles square) as may, by Cession of particular States, and the Acceptance of Congress, become the Seat of the Government of the United States, and to exercise like Authority over all Places purchased by the Consent of the Legislature of the State in which the Same shall be, for the Erection of Forts, Magazines, Arsenals, dock-Yards, and other needful Buildings; - And

To make all Laws which shall be necessary and proper for carrying into Execution the foregoing Powers, and all other Powers vested by this Constitution in the Government of the United States, or in any Department or Officer thereof.

Section. 9. The Migration or Importation of such Persons as any of the States now existing shall think proper to admit, shall not be prohibited by the Congress prior to the Year one thousand eight hundred and eight, but a Tax or duty may be imposed on such Importation, not exceeding ten dollars for each Person.

The Privilege of the Writ of Habeas Corpus shall not be suspended, unless when in Cases of Rebellion or Invasion the public Safety may require it.

No Bill of Attainder or ex post facto Law shall be passed.

No Capitation, or other direct, Tax shall be laid, [unless in Proportion to the Census or enumeration herein before directed to be taken].[5]

No Tax or Duty shall be laid on *Articles exported from any State.*

No Preference shall be given by any Regulation of Commerce or Revenue to the Ports of one State over those of another; nor shall Vessels bound to, or from, one State, be obliged to enter, clear, or pay Duties in another.

No Money shall be drawn from the Treasury, but in Consequence of Appropriations made by law; and a regular Statement and Account of the Receipts and Expenditures of all public Money shall be published from time to time.

No Title of *Nobility* shall be granted by the United States: and no Person holding any Office of Profit or Trust under them, shall, without the Consent of the Congress, accept of any present, Emolument, Office, or Title, of any kind whatever, from any King, Prince, or foreign State.

Section. 10. *No State* shall enter into any *Treaty*, Alliance, or Confederation; grant Letters of Marque and Reprisal; coin Money; emit Bills of Credit; make any Thing but *gold and silver Coin* a Tender in Payment of Debts; pass any Bill of Attainder, ex post facto Law, or Law impairing the Obligation of Contracts, or grant any Title of Nobility.

No State shall, without the Consent of the Congress, lay any *Imposts* or Duties on Imports or Exports, except what may be absolutely necessary for executing its inspection Laws: and the net Produce of all Duties and Imposts, laid by any State on Imports or Exports, shall be for the Use of the Treasury of the United States; and all such Laws shall be subject to the Revision and Control of the Congress.

No State shall, without the Consent of Congress, lay any Duty of Tonnage, keep Troops, or Ships of War in time of Peace, enter into any Agreement or Compact with another State, or with a foreign Power, or engage in War, unless actually invaded, or in such imminent Danger as will not admit of delay.

Article. II.

Section. 1. The ***executive*** Power shall be vested in a President of the United States of America. He shall hold his Office during the Term of four Years, and, together with the Vice President, chosen for the same Term, be elected, as follows:

Each State shall appoint, in such Manner as the Legislature thereof may direct, a Number of Electors, equal to the whole Number of Senators and Representatives to which the State may be entitled in the Congress: but no Senator or Representative, or Person holding an Office of Trust or Profit under the United States, shall be appointed an Elector. **(ADDED: Electors will be selected by name, not by affiliation with a Presidential candidate nor political party.)**

[The Electors shall meet in their respective States, **(ADDED: There shall be no national political party convention to determine Elector's votes)** and vote by Ballot for two Persons, of whom one at least shall not be an Inhabitant of the same State with themselves. And they shall make a List of all the Persons voted for, and of the Number of Votes for each, which ***List they shall sign and certify, and transmit sealed to the Seat of the Government of the United States, directed to the President of the Senate.*** The President of the Senate shall, in the Presence of the Senate and House of

Representatives, open all the Certificates, and the Votes shall then be counted. The *Person having the greatest Number of Votes shall be the President*, if such Number be a Majority of the whole Number of Electors appointed; and if there be more than one who have such Majority, and have an equal Number of Votes, then the House of Representatives shall immediately chuse by Ballot one of them for President; and if no Person have a Majority, then from the five highest on the List the said House shall in like Manner chuse the President. But in chusing the President, the Votes shall be taken by States, the Representation from each State having one Vote; A quorum for this purpose shall consist of a Member or Members from two thirds of the States, and a Majority of all the States shall be necessary to a Choice. In every Case, *after the Choice of the President, the Person having the greatest Number of Votes of the Electors shall be the Vice President.* But if there should remain two or more who have equal Vote, the Senate shall chuse from them by Ballot the Vice President.][6]

The Congress may determine the Time of chusing the Electors, and the Day on which they shall give their Votes; which Day shall be the same throughout the United States.

No Person except **a natural born Citizen**, **(ADDED: Natural Born Citizen is defined as being born of two persons who were US citizens at the time of the birth)** or a Citizen of the United States, at the time of the Adoption of this Constitution, shall be eligible to the Office of President; neither shall any Person be eligible to that Office who shall not have attained to the Age of thirty five Years, **and been fourteen Years a Resident within the United States**.

[In Case of the *Removal of the President* from Office, or of his Death, Resignation, or Inability to discharge the Powers and Duties of the said Office, the Same shall devolve on the Vice president, and the Congress may by law provide for the Case of Removal, Death, Resignation or Inability, both of the President and Vice President, declaring what Officer shall then act as President, and such Officer shall act accordingly, until the Disability be removed, or a President shall be elected.][7]

The President shall, at stated Times, receive for his Services, a Compensation, which shall neither be increased nor diminished during the Period for which he shall have been elected, and he shall not receive within that Period any other Emolument from the United States, or any of them.

Before he enter on the Execution of his Office, he shall take the following *Oath* or Affirmation: - *"I do solemnly swear (or affirm) that I will faithfully execute the Office of President of the United States, and will to the best of my Ability, preserve, protect and defend the Constitution of the United States."*

Section. 2. The President shall be *Commander in Chief* of the Army and Navy of the United States, and of the Militia of the several States, when called into
the actual Service of the United States; he may require the Opinion, in writing, of the principal Office in each of the executive Departments upon any Subject relating to the Duties of their respective Offices, and he shall have Power to grant Reprieves and Pardons for Offences against the United States, except in Cases of Impeachment.

He shall have Power, by and *with the Advice and Consent of the Senate*, to make Treaties provided two thirds of the Senators present concur, and he shall nominate, and by and with the Advice and Consent of the Senate, shall appoint Ambassadors, other public ministers and Consuls, Judges of the supreme court, and all other Officers of the United States, whose Appointments are not herein otherwise provided for, and which shall be established by Law: but the Congress may by Law vest the Appointment of such inferior Officers, as they think proper, in the President alone, in the Courts of Law; or in the Heads of Departments.

The President shall have Power to fill up all *Vacancies* that may happen *during the Recess of the Senate*, by granting Commissions which shall expire at the End of their next *Session*.

Section. 3. He shall from time to time give to the Congress Information of the State of the Union, and recommend to their Consideration such Measures as he shall judge necessary and expedient (Added: executive orders impacting law or the interpretation of law will expire after 30 days, unless affirmed by the appropriate Legislative or Judicial Branch); he may, on extraordinary Occasions, convene both Houses, or either of them, and in Case of Disagreement between them, with Respect to the Time of Adjournment, he may adjourn them to such Time as he shall think proper; he shall receive Ambassadors and other public ministers; *he shall take Care that the Laws be faithfully executed*, and shall Commission all the Officers of the United States.

Section. 4. The president, Vice President and all civil Officers of the United States, shall be removed from Office on impeachment for, and Conviction of, Treason, Bribery, or other high Crimes and Misdemeanors.

Article III.

Section. 1. The judicial Power of the United States shall be vested in one Supreme Court, *and in such inferior Courts as the Congress may from time to time ordain and establish.* The Judges, both of the supreme and inferior Courts, shall hold their Offices *during good Behaviour,* and shall, at stated Times, receive for their Services a Compensation, which shall not be diminished during their Continuance in Office.

Section. 2. The judicial Power shall extend to all Cases, in Law and Equity, arising under this Constitution, the Laws of the United States, and Treaties made, or which shall be made, under their Authority; - to All Cases affecting Ambassadors, other public Ministers and Consuls; - to all Cases of admiralty and maritime Jurisdiction; - to Controversies to which the United States shall be a Party; - to Controversies between two or more States; - [between a State and Citizens of another State;][8]- *between Citizens of different States;* - between Citizens of the same State claiming Lands under Grants of different States, [and between a State, or the Citizens thereof, and foreign States, Citizens or Subjects.]⁹

In all Cases affecting Ambassadors, other public Ministers and Consuls, and those in which a State shall be Party, the supreme Court shall have original Jurisdiction. In all the other Cases before mentioned, the supreme Court shall have appellate Jurisdiction, both as to Law and Fact, with such Exceptions, and under such Regulations as the Congress shall make.

The Trial of all Crimes, except in Cases of Impeachment, shall be by Jury; and such Trial shall be held in the State where the said Crimes shall have been committed; but when not committed within any State, the Trial shall be at such Place or Places as the Congress may by Law have directed.

Section. 3. *Treason* against the United States, shall consist only in levying War against them, or in adhering to their Enemies, giving them Aid and Comfort. No Person shall be convicted of Treason unless on the Testimony of two Witnesses to the same overt Act, or in Confession in open court.

The Congress shall have Power to declare the Punishment of Treason, but no Attainder of Treason shall work Corruption of Blood, or Forfeiture except during the Life of the Person attainted.

Article. IV.

Section. 1. Full Faith and Credit shall be given in each State to the public Acts, Records, and judicial Proceedings of every other State. And the congress may by general Laws prescribe the Manner in which such Acts, Records and Proceedings shall be proved, and the Effect thereof.

Section. 2. *The Citizens of each State shall be entitled to all Privileges and Immunities of Citizens in the several States.*

A Person charged in any State with Treason, Felony, or other Crime, who shall fell from Justice, and be found in another State, shall on Demand of the executive Authority of the State from which he fled, be delivered up, to be removed to the State having Jurisdiction of the Crime.

[No Person held to Service or Labour in one State, under the Laws thereof, escaping into another, shall, in Consequence of any Law or Regulation therein, be discharged from such Service or Labour, but shall be delivered up on Claim of the Party to whom such Service or Labour may be due.][10]

Section. 3. New States may be admitted by the Congress into this Union; but no new State shall be formed or erected within the Jurisdiction of any other State;
nor any State be formed by the Junction of two or more States, or Parts of States, without the Consent of the Legislatures of the States concerned as well as of the Congress.

The Congress shall have Power to dispose of and make all needful Rules and Regulations respecting the Territory or other Property belonging to the United States; and nothing in this Constitution shall be so construed as to Prejudice any Claims of the United States, or of *any particular State*.

Section. 4. The United States shall guarantee to every State in this Union a *Republican* **form of Government**, and shall protect each of them against Invasion; and on Application of the Legislature, or of the Executive (when the Legislature cannot be convened), against domestic Violence.

Article. V.

The Congress, whenever *two thirds of both Houses* shall deem it necessary, shall propose *Amendments* **to this Constitution**, or, on the Application of the Legislatures of **two thirds of the several States**, shall call a Convention for proposing Amendments, which, in either Case, shall be valid to all Intents and Purposes, as Part of this Constitution, when ratified by the Legislatures of *three fourths of the several States* or by Conventions in three fourths thereof, as the one or the other Mode of ratification may be proposed by the Congress; Provided that no Amendment which may be made prior to the Year One thousand eight hundred and eight shall in any Manner affect the first and fourth Clauses in the Ninth Section of the first Article; and that no State, without its Consent, shall be deprived of its equal Suffrage in the Senate.

Article. VI.

All Debts contracted and Engagements entered into, before the Adoption of this Constitution, shall be as valid against the United States under this Constitution, as under the Confederation.

This Constitution, and the *Laws of the United States which shall be made in Pursuance thereof; and all Treaties made, or which shall be made, under the Authority of the United States,* **shall be the supreme Law of the Land;** and the Judges in every State shall be bound thereby, any Thing in the Constitution or Laws of any State to the Contrary notwithstanding.

The Senators and Representatives before mentioned, and the Members of the several State Legislatures, and **all executive and judicial Officers, both of the United States and of the several States, shall be bound by Oath or Affirmation, to support this Constitution, but no religious Test shall ever be required** as a Qualification to any Office or public Trust under the United States.

Article. VII.

The Ratification of the conventions of nine States, shall be sufficient for the Establishment of this Constitution between the States so ratifying the Same.

Done in convention by the Unanimous Consent of the States present the Seventeenth Day of September in the Year of our Lord one thousand seven hundred and Eighty seven and of the Independence of the United States of America the Twelfth In witness whereof We have hereunto subscribed our Names,

Signed; G°. Washington
Presidt and deputy from Virginia
And others...

Notes:

[1] Changed by Section 2 of the Fourteenth Amendment.
[2] Changed by the Seventeenth Amendment.
[3] Changed by the Seventeenth Amendment.
[4] Changed by section 2 of the Twentieth Amendment.
[5] See Sixteenth Amendment.
[6] Changed by the Twelfth Amendment.
[7] Changed by the Twenty-Fifth Amendment.
[8] Changed by the Eleventh Amendment.
[9] Changed by the Thirteenth Amendment.

AMENDMENTS TO THE CONSTITUTION
OF THE UNITED STATES

Amendment I[1]

Congress shall make no law respecting an establishment of *religion*, or prohibiting the free exercise thereof; or abridging the freedom of *speech*, or of the *press*; or the right of the people peaceable to assemble, and to petition the Government for a redress of grievances.

Amendment II

A well regulated Militia, being necessary to the security of a free State, *the right of the people to keep and bear Arms, shall not be infringed.*

Amendment III

No Soldier shall, in time of peace be quartered in any house without the consent of the Owner, nor in time of war, but in a manner to be prescribed by law.

Amendment IV

The right of the people to be secure in their persons, houses, papers, and effects, against *unreasonable searches* and seizures, shall not be violated, and no Warrants shall issue, but upon *probable cause*, supported by Oath or affirmation, and particularly describing the place to be searched, and the persons or things to be seized.

Amendment V

No person shall be held to answer for a capital, or otherwise infamous crime, unless on a presentment or indictment of a Grand Jury, except in cases arising in the land or naval forces, or in the Militia, when in actual service in time of War or public danger; nor shall any person be subject for the same offence to be *twice* put in jeopardy of life or limb; nor shall be compelled in any criminal case to be a *witness against himself*, nor be deprived of life, liberty, or property, without due process of law; nor shall private property be taken for public use, without just compensation.

Amendment VI

In all criminal prosecutions, the accused shall enjoy the right to a *speedy and public trial*, by an impartial jury of the State and district wherein the crime shall have been committed, which district shall have been previously ascertained by law, and to be informed of the nature and cause of the accusation; to be confronted with the witnesses against him; to have compulsory process for obtaining witnesses in his favor, and to have the Assistance of *Counsel* for his defence.

Amendment VII

In Suits at common law, where the value in controversy shall exceed twenty dollars, the right of *trial by jury* shall be preserved, and no fact tried by a jury, shall be otherwise re-examined in any court of the United States, than according to the rules of the common law.

Amendment VIII

Excessive *bail* shall not be required, nor **excessive fines** imposed, nor cruel and unusual punishments inflicted. (Added: Monetary settlements will be limited to damages incurred. Punishment will not include other monetary awards to a plaintiff.)

Amendment IX

The *enumeration* in the Constitution, of certain rights, shall not be construed to deny or disparage others **retained by the people.**

Amendment X

The *powers not delegated to the United States by the Constitution*, nor prohibited by it to the States, are **reserved to the States** respectively, or to the people.

Amendment XI[2]

The Judicial power of the United States shall not be construed to extend to any suit in law or equity, commenced or prosecuted against one of the United States by Citizens of another State, or by Citizens or Subjects of any Foreign State.

Amendment XII[3]

The **Electors shall meet in their respective states** and vote by ballot for president and Vice-President, one of whom, at least, shall not be an inhabitant of the same state with themselves; **they shall name in their ballots the person voted for as President, and in <u>distinct ballots</u> the person voted for as Vice-President**, and they shall make distinct lists of all persons voted for as President, and of all persons voted for as Vice-President, and of the number of votes for each, which lists they shall sign and certify, and *transmit sealed to the seat of the government of the United States,* **directed to the President of the Senate**; - the President of the Senate shall, in the presence of the Senate and House of Representatives, open all the certificates and the votes shall then be counted; - The person having the greatest number of votes for President, shall be the President, if such number be a majority of the whole number of Electors appointed; and if no person have such majority, then from the persons having the highest numbers not exceeding three on the list of those voted for as President, the House of Representatives shall choose immediately, by ballot, the President. But in choosing the President, the votes **shall be taken by states**, the representation from each state having one vote; a quorum for this purpose shall consist of a member or members from two-thirds of the states, and a majority of all the states shall be necessary to a choice. [And if the House of Representatives shall not choose a President whenever the right of choice shall devolve upon them, before the fourth day of March next following, then the Vice-President shall act as President, as in case of the death or other constitutional disability of the President. -][4] The person having the greatest number of votes as Vice-President, shall be the Vice-President, if such number be a majority of the whole number of Electors appointed, and if no person have a majority, then from the two highest numbers on the list, the Senate shall choose the Vice-President; a quorum for the purpose shall consist of two-thirds of the whole number of Senators, and a majority of the whole number shall be necessary to a choice. ***But no person constitutionally ineligible to the office of President shall be eligible to that of Vice-President of the United States.***

Amendment XIII[5]

Section 1. Neither *slavery* nor involuntary servitude, except as a punishment for crime whereof the party shall have been duly convicted, shall exist within the United States, or any place subject to their jurisdiction.

Section 2. Congress shall have power to enforce this article by appropriate legislation.

Amendment XIV[6]

Section 1. All persons born or naturalized in the United States, and subject to the jurisdiction thereof, are citizens of the United States and of the State wherein they reside. No State shall make or enforce any law which shall abridge the privileges or immunities of citizens of the United States; nor shall any State deprive any person of life, liberty, or property, without due process of law; nor deny to any person within its jurisdiction the *equal protection* of the laws.

Section 2. Representatives shall be apportioned among the several States according to their respective numbers, counting the whole number of persons in each State, *excluding Indians not taxed.* But when the right to vote at any election for the choice of electors for President and Vice-President of the United States, Representatives in Congress, the Executive and Judicial officers of a State, or the members of the Legislature thereof, is denied to any of the *male* inhabitants of such State, being twenty-one years of age, and citizens of the United States, or in any way abridged, except for participation in rebellion, or other crime, the basis of representation therein shall be reduced in the proportion which the number of such male citizens shall bear to the whole number of male citizens twenty-one years of age in such State.

Section 3. No person shall be a Senator or Representative in Congress, or elector of President and Vice-President, or hold any office, civil or military, under the United States, or under any State, who having previously taken an oath, as a member of Congress, or as an officer of the United States, or as a member of any State legislature, or as an executive or judicial officer of any State, to support the Constitution of the United States, shall have engaged in insurrection or rebellion
against the same, or given aid or comfort to the enemies thereof. But congress may by a vote of two-thirds of each House, remove such disability.

Section 4. The validity of the public debt of the United States, authorized by law, including debts incurred for payment of pensions and bounties for services in suppressing insurrection or rebellion shall not be questioned. But neither the United States nor any State shall assume or pay any debt or obligation incurred in
aid of insurrection or rebellion against the United States, or any claim for the loss or emancipation of any slave; but all such debts, obligations and claims shall be held illegal and void.

Section 5. The Congress shall have the power to enforce, by appropriate legislation, the provisions of this article.

Amendment XV[7]

Section 1. The right of citizens of the United States to vote shall not be denied or abridged by the United States or by any State on account of *race*, color, or previous condition of servitude –

Section 2. The Congress shall have the power to enforce this article by appropriate legislation.

Amendment XVI[8]

The Congress shall **(ADDED: not)** have power to lay and collect *taxes on incomes*, ~~from whatever source derived, without apportionment among the several States, and without regard to any census or enumeration.~~ **(ADDED: The FairTax shall be the only source of federal income to be derived from the citizens.**

Amendment XVII[9]

The ***Senate*** of the United States shall be composed ***of*** ~~two~~ *(ADDED: one)-*Senators~~from each State, *elected by the people thereof,* for *(ADDED: a single term of) six years*~~; and each Senator shall have one vote. The electors in each State shall have the qualifications requisite for electors of the most numerous branch of the State legislatures.

When vacancies happen in the representation of any State in the Senate, the executive authority of such State shall issue writs of election to fill such vacancies:
Provided, That the legislature of any State may empower the executive thereof to
make temporary appointments until the people fill the vacancies by election as the legislature may direct.

This amendment shall not be so construed as to affect the election or term of any Senator chosen before it becomes valid as part of the Constitution.

Amendment XVIII[10]

Section 1. After one year from the ratification of this article the manufacture, sale, or transportation of intoxicating *liquors* within, the importation thereof into, or the exportation thereof from the United States and all territory subject to the jurisdiction thereof for beverage purposes is hereby prohibited.

Section 2. The Congress and the several States shall have concurrent power to enforce this article by appropriate legislation.

Section 3. This article shall be inoperative unless it shall have been ratified as an amendment to the Constitution by the legislatures of the several States, as provided in the Constitution, within seven years from the date of the submission hereof to the States by the Congress.

Amendment XIX[11]

The right of citizens of the United States to vote shall not be denied or abridged by the United States or by any State on account of *sex.*

Congress shall have power to enforce this article by appropriate legislation.

Amendment XX[12]

Section 1. The terms of the President and the Vice President shall end at noon on the 20th day of January, and the terms of Senators and Representatives at noon on the 3d day of January, of the years in which such terms would have ended if this article had not been ratified; and the terms of their successors shall then begin.

Section 2. The Congress shall assemble at least once in every year, and such meeting shall begin at noon on the 3d day of January, unless they shall by law appoint a different day.

Section 3. If, at the time fixed for the beginning of the term of the President, the President elect shall have died, the Vice President elect shall become President. If a President shall not have been chosen before the time fixed for the beginning of his term, or if the President elect shall have failed to qualify, then the Vice President elect shall act as President until a President shall have qualified; and the Congress may by law provide for the case wherein neither a President elect nor a Vice President shall have qualified, declaring who shall then act as President, or the manner in which one who is to act shall be selected, and such person shall act accordingly until a President or Vice President shall have qualified.

Section 4. The Congress may by law provide for the case of the death of any of the persons from whom the House of Representatives may choose a President whenever the right of choice shall have devolved upon them, and for the case of the death of any of the persons from whom the senate may choose a Vice President whenever the right of choice shall have devolved upon them.

Section 5. Sections 1 and 2 shall take effect on the 15th day of October following the ratification of this article.

Section 6. This article shall be inoperative unless it shall have been ratified as an amendment to the Constitution by the legislatures of three-fourths of the several States within seven years from the date of its submission.

Amendment XXI[13]

Section 1. The eighteenth article of amendment to the Constitution of the United States is hereby repealed.

Section 2. The transportation or importation into any State, Territory, or Possession of the United States for delivery or use therein of intoxicating *liquors*, violation of the laws thereof, is hereby prohibited.

Section 3. This article shall be inoperative unless it shall have been ratified as an amendment to the Constitution by conventions in the several States as provided in the Constitution, within seven years from the date of the submission hereof to the States by the Congress.

Amendment XXII[14]

~~Section 1.~~ No person shall be elected to **(ADDED: any federal office)** ~~the office of the President~~ *more than* ~~twice~~, *(Added: once((possible alternative: twice)); terms of office of President, Senator and Representative will be six years)* ~~and no person who has held the office of President, or acted as President, for more than two years of a term to which some other person was elected President shall be elected to the office of President more than once. But this Article shall not apply to any person holding the office of President when this Article was proposed by congress, and shall not prevent any person who may be holding the office of President, or acting as President, during the term within which this Article becomes operative from holding the office of President or acting as President during the remainder of such term.~~

~~Section 2. This article shall be inoperative unless it shall have been ratified as an amendment to the Constitution by the legislatures of three-fourths of the several States within seven years from the date of its submission to the States by the Congress.~~

Amendment XXIII[15]

Section 1. *The District* constituting the seat of Government of the United States shall appoint in such manner as Congress may direct:

A number of electors of President and Vice President equal to the whole number of Senators and Representatives in Congress to which the District would be entitles if it were a State, but in no event more than the least populous State; they shall be in addition to those appointed by the States, but they shall be considered, for the purposes of the election of President and Vice President, to be electors appointed by a State, and they shall meet in the District and perform such duties as provided by the twelfth article of amendment.

Section 2. The Congress shall have power to enforce this article by appropriate legislation.

Amendment XXIV[16]

Section 1. The right **of citizens** of the United States to vote in any primary or other election for President or Vice President, for electors for President or Vice President, or for Senator or Representative in Congress, shall not be denied or abridged by the United States or any State by reason of failure to pay *poll tax* or other tax.

(ADDED: Section 2. However, positive proof of U.S, citizenship and proof of passing the U.S. Citizenship exam are required to vote in any State or National election.)

Section 2̶ (ADDED: 3). The Congress shall have power to enforce this article by appropriate legislation.

Amendment XXV[17]

Section 1. In case of the *removal of the President* from office or of his death or resignation, the Vice President shall become President.

Section 2. Whenever there is a vacancy in the office of the Vice president, the President shall nominate a Vice President who shall take office upon confirmation by a majority vote of both Houses of Congress.

Section 3. Whenever the President transmits to the President pro tempore of the Senate and the Speaker of the House of Representatives his written declaration that he is unable to discharge the powers and duties of his office, and until he transmits to them a written declaration to the contrary, such powers and duties shall be discharged by the Vice President as Acting president.

Section 4. Whenever the Vice President and a majority of either the principal officers of the executive departments or of such other body as Congress may by law provide, transmit to the President pro tempore of the Senate and the Speaker of the House of representatives their written declaration that the President is unable to discharge the powers and duties of his office, the Vice President shall immediately assume the powers and duties of the office as Acting President.

Thereafter, when the President transmits to the President pro tempore of the Senate and the Speaker of the

House of Representatives his written declaration that no inability exists, he shall resume the powers and duties of his office unless the Vice President and a majority of either the principal officers of the executive
department or of such other body as Congress may by law provide, transmit within
four days to the President pro tempore of the Senate and the Speaker of the House of representatives their written declaration that the President is unable to discharge the powers and duties of his office. Thereupon Congress shall decide the issue, assembling within forty-eight hours for that purpose if not in session. If the Congress, within twenty-one days after receipt of the latter written declaration, or, if Congress is not in session, within twenty-one days after Congress is required to assemble, determines by two-thirds vote of both Houses that the President is unable to discharge the powers and duties of his office, the Vice President shall continue to discharge the same as Acting President; otherwise the President shall resume the powers and duties of his office.

Amendment XXVI[18]

~~Section 1. The right of citizens of the United States, who are *eighteen years of age* or older, to vote shall not be denied or abridged by the United States or by any State on account of age.~~
~~Section 2. the Congress shall have power to enforce this article by appropriate legislation.~~

Amendment XXVII[19]

No law, varying the *compensation* for the services of the Senators and Representatives, shall take effect, until an election of representatives shall have intervened.

(ADDED: Amendment XXVIII)

Voter Integrity. To ensure that the American voter gets the leadership it wants and deserves, an informed and legitimate electorate is required.

Section 1. A test of voter comprehension will consist of a computer-generated random selection of ten (10) questions from the standard US Citizenship exam required of newly Naturalized US citizens. A passing grade of 70% is required to be eligible to vote.

Section 2. Valid proof of US citizenship is required to be eligible to vote. A US birth certificate or passport or notarized validation witnessed by three (3) certified US citizens is required.

Section 3. The right to vote of citizens of the United States who are twenty-five years of age or older shall not be denied or abridged by the United States or by any State on account of age.

(ADDED: Amendment XXIX)

Balance of Power. Each of the branches, Executive, Legislative and Judicial, shall review all actions of the other branches. When one branch challenges an action of another, the third branch will be the arbitrator. A simple majority created by the arbitrator will be final.

(ADDED: Amendment XXX)

Tenure of Federal Couort Justices. Federal Court Justices including members of the Supreme Court will have a maximum term of 20 years and maximum age of 80 years of age. (Alternative wording, "Federal Court Justices including Supreme Court justices will be appointed to a term of 6 years, with a limit of one re-appointment by the appointing authority in office at the time of the re-appointment.")

Notes:

[1]   The first ten Amendments (Bill of Rights) were ratified effective December 15, 1791.
[2]   The Eleventh Amendment was ratified February 7, 1795.
[3]   The Twelfth Amendment was ratified June 15, 1804.
[4]   Superseded by section 3 of the Twentieth Amendment.
[5]   The Thirteenth Amendment was ratified December 6, 1865.
[6]   The fourteenth Amendment was ratified July 9, 1868.
[7]   The Fifteenth Amendment was ratified February 3, 1870.
[8]   The Sixteenth Amendment was ratified February 3, 1913.
[9]   The Seventeenth Amendment was ratified April 8, 1913.
[10]   The Eighteenth Amendment was ratified January 16, 1919. It was repealed by the Twenty-First Amendment December 5, 1933.
[11]   The nineteenth Amendment was ratified August 18, 1920.
[12]   The Twentieth Amendment was ratified January 23, 1933.
[13]   The Twenty-First Amendment was ratified December 5, 1933.
[14]   The Twenty-Second Amendment was ratified February 27, 1951.
[15]   The Twenty-Third Amendment was ratified March 29, 1961.
[16]   The Twenty-Fourth Amendment was ratified January 23, 1964.
[17]   The Twenty-Fifth Amendment was ratified February 10, 1967.

[18] The Twenty-Sixth Amendment was ratified July 1, 1971.

[19] The Twenty-Seventh Amendment was ratified May 7, 1992.

Annex I

America's Plan for Survival:

PART TWO,
CURRENT ISSUES

ANNEXES

(The book can be purchased on Amazon.com,
or Createspace.com or by contacting the author at
hanksims@apfsbook.com.)